cloverleaf books™

Money Basics

Ella Earns Her Own Money

Lisa Bullard

illustrated by Mike Moran

M MILLBROOK PRESS • MINNEAPOLIS

To Laura —L.B.
To Matthew —M.M.

Millbrook Press
A division of Lerner Publishing Group, Inc.
241 First Avenue North
Minneapolis, MN 55401 USA

For reading levels and more information,
look up this title at www.lernerbooks.com.

Main body text set in Slappy Inline 18/28.
Typeface provided by T26.

Library of Congress Cataloging-in-Publication Data

Bullard, Lisa.
    Ella earns her own money / by Lisa Bullard ; illustrated by
Mike Moran.
        p.   cm. — (Cloverleaf books™—money basics)
    Includes index.
    ISBN 978–1–4677–0761–9 (lib. bdg. : alk. paper)
    ISBN 978–1–4677–1693–2 (EB pdf)
    1. Moneymaking projects for children—Juvenile literature.
2. Money—Juvenile literature. 3. Work—Juvenile literature.
4. Finance, Personal—Juvenile literature. I. Moran, Michael,
1957– II. Title.
HF5392.B85 2014
650.1'2083—dc23   2012037343

Manufactured in the United States of America
2-44120-12962-4/28/2017

TABLE OF CONTENTS

I Want That Soccer Ball!

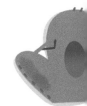

"Please can we buy it, Mom?" I asked.

"I need a new soccer ball!"

"You already have one," Mom replied.
"That ball costs $20.00. We'll talk about it tonight."

After dinner, Mom handed me a dollar bill and four quarters. "An allowance will help you learn about saving and spending," she said. Now I'll have my own money. As soon as I have $20.00, I can buy that soccer ball myself.

Three of my quarters are to save. We will bring them to the bank. One quarter is to donate. I want to give it to places that help animals. The rest is to spend. Or to **save up for something special.**

Save

Share

Spend

AMOUNT IN ELLA'S SPEND JAR:
$1.00

Chapter Two

Working for Money

I dusted Monday morning. That's one of my chores. My friend Will has chores too. That's how he earns his allowance. But Mom said we do it differently at our house. Here chores are just part of being in our family.

Set table
Clean room
✓Dust
Feed fish

AMOUNT IN ELLA'S SPEND JAR:
$1.00+$1.00=$2.00

TRASH

I kept thinking about that soccer ball. I needed $19.00 more. Mom said she would pay me for doing special jobs. So I cleaned out the car and she gave me $1.00. I wonder who left all that stuff in there.

Then Mom helped me make posters. They said,
"Hire Ella!" We gave them to our neighbors.

The next day, Mr. Hanson asked me to weed. He paid me $2.00. Ms. Lowry paid me to give Barney a bath on Wednesday. **I got another $1.00.** And a free bath!

AMOUNT IN ELLA'S SPEND JAR:
$2.00+$2.00+$1.00=$5.00

On Thursday, Aiden's mom called. She paid me $2.00 to keep Aiden busy while she worked. We played with my old soccer ball. The new one would have been more fun.

Saving money takes so long! When we finished, Aiden's mom gave me an extra **$1.00.** That was for cleaning up Aiden.

AMOUNT IN ELLA'S SPEND JAR:
$5.00+$2.00+$1.00=$8.00

Chapter Three

Buying and Selling

On Saturday, Will came over. He really wanted one of my old games. My mom said I could sell it to him if his dad said it was OK. Will gave me **$4.00** from his allowance savings.

After we dropped off Will, we stopped at the store. My favorite gum was only $1.00. Yum! Later, I counted my money again. I still needed $9.00. And the gum was already gone.

$1.00

GUM

AMOUNT IN ELLA'S SPEND JAR:
$8.00+$4.00-$1.00=$11.00

My babysitter taught me to make bracelets.
She even left me some supplies. So I made
two on Sunday.

AMOUNT IN ELLA'S SPEND JAR:
$11.00+$2.00+$2.00+$1.00=$16.00

Then I sold them to the twins next door. They paid me **$2.00** each. And I got my allowance again. That meant another **$1.00** for spending. But I still didn't have enough to buy that soccer ball.

Chapter Four

It All Adds Up

I called Grandma on Monday. I told her I'd been working hard. Guess what? She said she had a big job.

We cleaned her garage together. It took all afternoon. **She gave me a cookie.** And she paid me **$4.00!** Finally, I had **$20.00**. That was enough for my soccer ball.

AMOUNT IN ELLA'S SPEND JAR:
$16.00+$4.00=$20.00

Mom picked me up from Grandma's. "Are you ready to buy that soccer ball?" she asked.

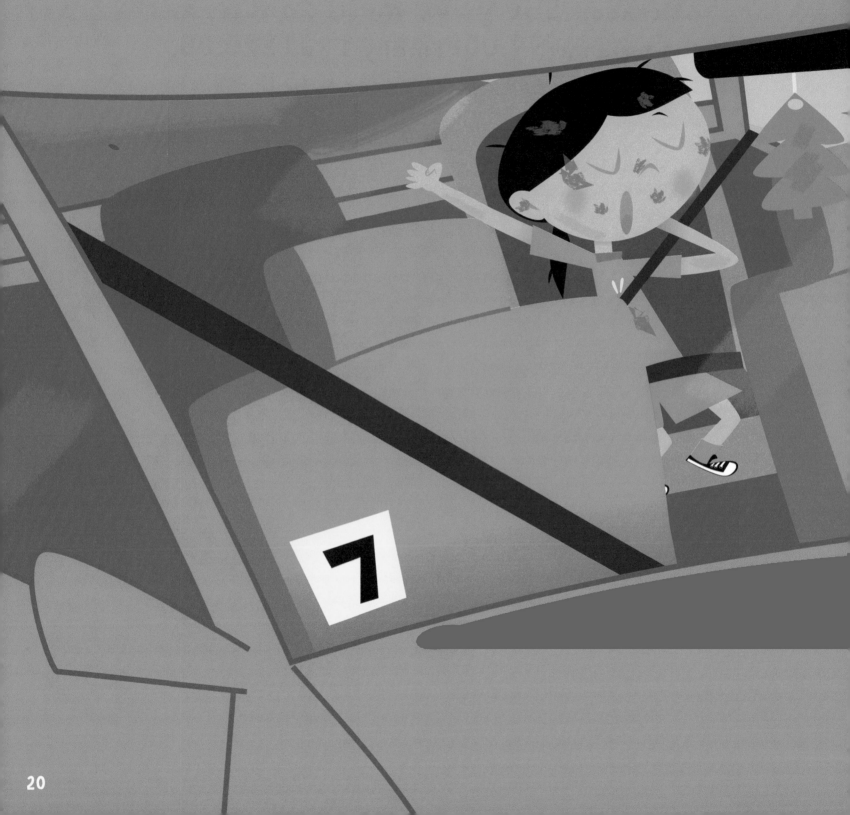

"Thanks, Mom," I said. "But I'm really tired from all this working! Could we shop tomorrow instead?"

Make a Money Chart

Are you saving your money for something special? It can be fun to keep track of how much you have saved! This chart will help you.

What you need:

printer paper   washable black marker
clear tape   green crayon

What you do:

1) Figure out how much money you need to earn to buy your special item. If it is not an even dollar amount, round up to the next highest dollar. That is your goal. Write your goal number on one corner of your paper.

2) Use the black marker to draw a rectangle on the paper. The rectangle should be about the size of a bandage.

3) Put the number "1" on that rectangle using the black marker.

4) Draw a second rectangle on the same sheet of paper. Put the number "2" on that rectangle.

5) Keep numbering rectangles: 3, 4, 5, 6, 7, and so on. Keep numbering until the number of rectangles matches the goal number you wrote in the corner of your paper.

6) If you run out of room on your first sheet of paper, keep numbering on another sheet of paper. Tape your sheets of paper together.

7) Now you have a money chart. Ask an adult where you can hang it.

8) When you earn your first dollar, color in the rectangle marked "1" using the green crayon. When you earn your second dollar, color in the rectangle marked "2."

9) Keep going until you have earned enough money to color in all your rectangles.

10) Buy your special item!

GLOSSARY

allowance: money paid to a person, often a child, on a regular basis

bank: a place to save money or to do other money business

chores: the everyday jobs that need to be done by a family

donate: to give money away, often to help people or animals

hire: to pay someone to work for you

BOOKS

Cleary, Brian P. *A Dollar, a Penny, How Much and How Many?* Minneapolis: Millbrook Press, 2012.
Rhyming text and goofy illustrations introduce U.S. bills and coins.

Larson, Jennifer S. *What Can You Do with Money?: Earning, Spending, and Saving.* Minneapolis: Lerner Publications Company, 2010.
This photo-illustrated book teaches you more about how people earn money.

Salzmann, Mary Elizabeth. *Money for Toys.* Edina, MN: Abdo, 2011.
Come along as Olivia learns about spending and saving.

Spinelli, Eileen. *Miss Fox's Class Earns a Field Trip.* Park Ridge, IL: Albert Whitman, 2010.
Follow along in this funny story as Miss Fox's class tries to earn money.

WEBSITES

It's My Life: Money
http://pbskids.org/itsmylife/money/index.html
Check out the Money section of this fun site from PBS. You'll find info on spending, making, and managing money.

Planet Orange
http://www.orangekids.com
This website from ING Direct lets you blast off to play games and learn more about earning and saving money.

Wise Pockets World
http://www.umsl.edu/~wpockets
This website has stories to help you learn more about earning money and buying things.

LERNER *e* SOURCE™
Expand learning beyond the printed book. Download free, complementary educational resources for this book from our website, www.lerneresource.com.